IN HER OWN WORDS

WORDS

An Encouraging Journey of
Courage and Bravery

Naomi Green Ward

CONTENTS

ACKNOWLEDGEMENTS

I would like to thank one of the most important people in my life, my husband, **William N. Ward, Jr.** From day one, you have been supportive of me. You are strength when I am weak. You have displayed your love for me in so many ways. You have tried to understand me and that is important to me. There were many times as I dealt with grief that you kept me motivated to write this book. You kept me on task by being a little worrisome at times to ensure that I met deadlines. Thank you for removing every excuse. You and your push are appreciated. I love you, Honey!

I thank my son, **Nathaniel L. Green, Sr.,** God's gift to me. From your first breath, you have been a blessing to me and have given me life. I cannot express the impact that your life has had on mine. You are my reason for it all. When I wanted to quit, I would look at you and realize that I couldn't. You make me want to be a better person. You are integral, genuine, and authentically you! I am thankful for your candor and unconditional love. Thanks for finding wonderful Kennisha, making her your wife (my daughter), and obtaining favor from the Lord. Together, you have both inspired me, prayed for me, and I get double the love. I thank you for your encouragement and being the rock that I needed to keep me going. Nothing can ever replace the time that we have together. There is no one like you! I love you, Nathaniel and Kennisha.

I thank my brother and sister, the late **Michael D. Green, Sr.** and the late **Norvice G. Sellers.** You were both very influential in my life, spiritually and naturally. Michael, you would check my spirit and remind me of the importance of my words. I still seek what God says about me above the words of others. Norvice, you encouraged me to seek God for a purpose-filled life and inner healing. You both shared your time, many words of wisdom, prayer, laughter, and encouragement. I love and miss you both beyond words!

To my sister, **Deborah Golden**, my words cannot describe who you are to me. You always know when I need to talk, when we need to pray, and when I need to be still. You are a woman of wisdom. You are my sister and best friend. It's a win-win. We went from dating together to doing ministry together. You have always been honest with me. Life happens, people change, but I pray that what we have will always remain. You are the real deal. You know me and I want you to know that I love you!

My siblings are just awesome! Thank you, **Jacquelin Holmes, Dwight Green, Sr., Samuel Green, III, Natalie Neal, and Phillip Green, Sr.** We are family! Although some of our family members have passed, we are still together, and that is important. We are jointly fit together with the comfort and ease of a hand in a well-fit glove. As Ephesians 4:16 says, we are joined together and compacted by that which every joint supplieth, according to the effectual working in the measure of every part, maketh increase of the body unto the edifying of itself in love. It is from Christ that the whole body grows as each different part does its work. Each of you have contributed to my growth and who I am today. Thank you big time. I love y'all!!!!

Thank you to my extended **Green family.** I love all of my nieces and nephews, but **JR, Marcus, Benjamin, PJ,** and **Lauren,** you are like my own children. You have allowed me to be a part of your lives. When I moved away, you kept in touch and I cherish our time together. As you have grown, our relationship has also. There is a chemistry and connection within our family unit for which I am grateful. I never know what's going to happen when our family gets together, but I can be sure there will be food, songs, laughter, and prayer. I love my family!

Ward family, thank you for your open arms and support. I have enjoyed becoming a member of the family. It's definitely a God thing.

Thank you to my Publisher, **Adrienne E. Bell.** I know that authors like me can make you want to stop publishing. I know that I may have made this project a challenge for you, but you hung in there with me.

DEDICATION

I dedicate this book to my parents, **Madam Vivian F.** and **Bishop Samuel L. Green, Jr.**

The most loving, kind people I know. The best part of my life was you. I never thought I would be doing life without you. My mother, always had faith in me, even when I did not have faith in mysef. She pushed me beyond the limits that I placed on myself. I am aspiring to be the woman that she saw I could be. My dad showed me what faith in God looks like, against all odds. Mom and Dad, I can sometimes hear your words of wisdom, inspiration, and encouragement. Thank you for your impartation. "I can do all things through Christ who strengthens me". No turning back. We got this!

FOREWORD

This woman knows what to do when life seems to explode. She can show you how to put the pieces back together. When things explode in her family, finances, and personal life, she always figures out how to put it back together with wisdom and grace.

Some explosions I witnessed and others I heard about. I think the biggest explosion was **me**. Nobody expected the Bishop's daughter to have a baby out of wedlock. He's a bigger-than-life figure; a holiness preacher. She's a hard worker in the church and has been all her life, so no one expected that. It was an explosion because your father is mad. After all, he's hurt; he's hurt because of what he wanted for your life. He's also hurt because, politically, it is unacceptable. Your mother is hurt, and then you have your siblings – some supportive and some judgemental. Their judgment mostly comes from what they think "Daddy" would want to hear. So, you have the family dynamic blowing up in your face.

Then, you have relationships you were building that had to change because you're pregnant now. People at the church were just being mean. Then again, my grandfather was very vocal, but some people behaved a certain way because they *thought* that's how he felt, so they just chimed in. People can be very fickle sometimes.

Then, they forget that this woman is a soul. Not only is she a soul, but she's carrying a soul. I remember my mom sharing with me, and I testify about it all the time now, how she was in the restroom while at home, she had a handful of pills. Something in her mind said, "You can take all of these right now and end all of your suffering." Holy Spirit said, "You don't realize what is in your belly." She immediately flushed all of the pills.

I can only imagine how dark of a place my mother was in, but one thing I can say is from the moment my eyes met hers, my mother never did anything to make me think that she regretted my being here.

Later in life, my grandfather phrased it best. He said, "It was the will of God for him to be here. *How* he got here wasn't the right way." But my mom, with all that she went through, never once made me feel as if I was a mistake, even though she made a mistake. Whatever God was ministering to my mother when she was carrying me was enough to get her through. The Comforter was getting her through because I know how mean some of the saints were. I know what was being said in the earlier years from the pulpit out of her father's hurt, and he didn't know how to express it in the best way.

I always felt the need to defend her all the time. That's my mom, and you want everybody to see your mother the way you see her. In my eyes, my mother can do no wrong; She is my hero. She is this amazing woman, and I can say this because she *has* done and she *is* doing things for me that she's never done for them, so they don't get to see what I see. All they get to do is judge from where they're sitting. I get to judge from what I'm experiencing.

I'm experiencing her bending over backwards to make sure that life is good for me, and I'm also seeing and experiencing her bending over backwards to make sure life is good for other people! That's one thing my mother has always bent over backwards to try to extend a level of help, love, and care to people who rarely bent over backwards to extend the same things to her.

The bravest thing she's ever done is raise me by herself. She had help with my grandparents, but initially, it was just me and her, and she did well. I never wanted for *anything*. It's funny. When I tell people about some of my struggles growing up, they ask *how* because my grandfather was a millionaire. Yes, I wish my mother would have taken advantage of his millions, however, my mom was determined to make it on her own without anyone's help.

When we went home to live with my grandparents, we didn't go back because she couldn't afford to live on our own, but I think it made better sense to raise me in an environment to ensure I developed the right way. Looking back, I think it made sense in that regard. It wasn't because Mama couldn't handle it. Mama took care of her and me and did a great job doing it. I think that was brave. She made it all happen and without the assistance of anybody.

My Grandfather would come over to the apartment in Lakeland Village and try to give her money. He would come in, talk to us, see how we were doing, and try to give her money, but she wouldn't take it. When I got older, I asked her, "Are you crazy? Why wouldn't you take that money?"

When my Grandfather saw that she wouldn't take it, he would give it to me and tell me to give it to her. My mother was determined to make it on her own. She never said this to me, but I believe her mindset was, "Let me see if I can make it without you because the moment that I see that I can, I'm going to show you that I can." She was determined to prove, "I can make it without you." I think it also gave a level of peace. When you're in somebody's pocket in their mind, it gives them a right to say what they want to say to you or about you. When they have no say about how you're being sustained, there isn't much they can say. All they can do is salute you because you're making it on your own.

Another brave thing my mother did was work hard in ministry. Anything my grandfather gave her to do in his church or his business, she did it with excellence. Even if he gave her a task she was not an expert in, she would figure it out. My mother has the spiritual gift of administration. She could supernaturally figure things out even if she had no experience. Back in those days, we called it a secretary. Over the years, we saw that secretaries were undervalued, so we gave them a better name, "administrators." As a pastor, I know how important it is to have a good administrator because if I didn't have one, I wouldn't have much of what I have. They make my world go 'round, and that's what Mama did. She was a great administrator and added tremendous value to my grandfather's ministry and business.

When my grandfather said, "I want you to take over the whole choir," and we're talking about a huge choir, she took it and did a great job with it. When he said, "I want you to take over this business." She took it and sustained it. That wasn't her forte, but anything he gave her to do, she took it and made it work. Mama receives an A+ in my book for her bravery.

I have tremendous respect for my mother because she is the blueprint that there is nothing you can be guilty of or fall into that is so horrible that it would eliminate God's will for your life. It may delay some things, but those things will not be denied to you because God will hold them together until you get yourself together. My mom's life is a testament that He waited for her to get herself together.

After I was born, looking at some of the relationships she entertained, I think they weren't the best relationships to be in. Still, she chose those relationships because they were an escape from all of the frustration that came along with mistakes that people won't let you forget. She was looking for love, acceptance, and laughter. These individuals put a smile on her face. Mom wasn't trying to do something ungodly or unrighteous. Still, some people fall into certain things, certain traps, and certain decisions because it is an escape from the consequences of other choices that they made that didn't turn out the way they thought they would. Even in those escapes, when she found herself more lost, the Lord found her and put her on the path He'd chosen for her.

When you finish reading this book, I want you to understand that nothing you can get involved in would eliminate God's plan for your life. It may delay it, but it is not denied. God has a plan for you. There's nothing that the enemy can throw at you that will stop God's plan.

Mama has mastered making lemonade out of lemons! I

can't tell you how many times I've told her, "You're better than me!" and she really is! I'm very, very, very, very proud of her.

To my Mom, I have enjoyed being able to sit close enough to read each chapter of your life that's not written in this book. I believe this book is going to be yet another chapter that the world gets a chance to benefit from. I'm super proud of you and excited about what God is about to do!

With Love From Your Only Son,
Nathaniel L. Green, Sr.

PROLOGUE

MICHAEL, MY ANGEL

I woke up on February 1, 2021, to a reality that I was not ready to accept. My heart was broken because my brother, my friend, my confidante was dead. A nice way to say it is that he passed. My reality was not as nice to me. He's dead! I found difficulty in saying those words. January 31, 2021, will forever be etched in my memory. I can remember the numbness I felt when I called to inquire about the status of my brother's health. To hear the confusion on the other end of the telephone caused me great anxiety as I attempted to arrest my emotions. When the words "He's gone" were uttered, complete disbelief overtook me. My knees almost buckled as I struggled to find a chair. How could he be gone? Someone has made a mistake. God has so much left for him to do! He can't be gone. I just talked to him and laughed with him. He told me he was on the mend. This cannot be my truth! I have lost my mother, my father, my niece, my sister, and now my brother. As I collected myself, I heard myself say, "He's gone"' and then "God why?" There would be no more heart-to-heart conversations. No more light humor from him. No more words of wisdom would fall from his lips to my ears. No longer am I able to pick up the phone to extract the true revelation of scripture from his perspective. Everything that he had imparted into my life must live on its own now through me. I had to hold onto what he had already given because there was to be no more life extended to me from this vessel that God had given to me. It is now my responsibility to remember what has been given and make good use of it. To apply it to my life.

In that moment I was tasked to remember. Remember the words of knowledge, the words of truth, the words of encouragement. I was reminded to appreciate the time that we did have together and cherish it. Remember his laughter, his strength, his thoughtfulness, his hurt, his healing. Those are some of the things that have helped me through my loss. Most importantly, I cried out to God for answers. I actually cried to God and I believe He heard me because He spoke clearly to me that Michael was a gift. His time for rest had come. Honestly, I didn't want to hear that but in the midst of my tears I realized that He is God and He knows what is best. With all of the questions I had, I accepted that my brother was not taken before his time, He was taken at God's specified time. God had given me a gift in the life of my family members and one by one, as they were being rewarded with rest, God was showing me the urgency of my assignment. We must work while it is day for the night cometh when no man can work. This verse of scripture is incredibly important because it contains a strong admonition for every serious Christian. God has given all of us time to do His works. I am to focus on what He has me here for as long as I am in the world and able to do what He has asked me to do. Night is the time for rest.

Just like night has come for others, night is coming for us. I am working as hard as I can, while I can.

After talking to God about Michael's passing, I thought about a lot of our conversations. My thoughts lingered on one in particular. I could remember when Michael shared prophetically with me. He spoke to me in the Spirit about the birthing of something new in my ministry. He described how I had helped everyone else while putting myself on the back burner and told me it was time for me. He said some other things but these words caused me to search deep inside myself. I started to recall some of the other words of prophecy that had been spoken over my life. After Michael gave me these eye-opening words, I began to think of what God had called me to do. When and how would I begin to let His works flow through me? When I sat with Michael again, just to gain deeper insight into what I thought God was telling me, he became excited about what God was going to do through me. He encouraged me to do it. To take the lead and run with what God was giving me to do.

He confirmed what another evangelist had spoken to me, that I would write. That was difficult for me to accept because if people don't want to hear what I have to say, why would they want to purchase a book to read what I have written? I had no intention of writing because I had no idea where to start. But when a publisher/friend contacted me with the same question, I thought it was time to write. Just start at the beginning. I contacted Michael with an idea (that is still in the works) and he encouraged me to keep him updated on my progress because he wanted to see it. He explained that the trick of the enemy was for me to never see my true potential. He died before I could complete the project but it did prompt me to start NEW Life which is a weekly FB Live conversation about life. NEW Life is Part 1 in the stages to complete the project. I came to understand that for a large portion of my life, I had focused on the negatives and what I thought people said and thought about me. I cannot tell you what a waste of time that is. He helped me to know that what is most important is what God is saying, "You are chosen". That's awesome because I went from being called to being chosen. Michael has always been a bright light and strong influence in my life, and he still is. I believe that thoughts about Michael inspire me. I have often thought about why my inspiration is Michael, but the why is what pushes me forward. Michael is my inspiration because he never judged me. With all that I was, he never judged me. I can hear him saying, "Naomi, now Naomi". Nothing more needed to be said. We were alike in a lot of ways. He always had an open hand extended to me. He always showered me with love and affection. He never changed, no matter my situation. He inspires me.

I am walking in my purpose and there is absolutely nothing like it!

IN MY OWN WORDS

Over forty years ago, someone told me I would become an author, and people wanted to hear what I had to say. I did not see God wanting to use *me* to help **anyone**. I felt inadequate and desired to stay in the background where I was comfortable. Four decades ago, I was not the person that I am today. I could not wrap my mind around the possibility of being an example for anyone, nor did I have confidence in my ability to help someone else through my written testimony. I could not have been more wrong.

Over the last two decades, many people have asked me when I was going to write a book. These inquiries caused me to realize that my voice needed to be heard because I had something valuable to offer.

This is not a tell-all book about my life but a testimony of God's faithfulness throughout my life. This practical guide is a clear roadmap to overcoming life's challenges when:

- *Accepting your identity*
- *Navigating through grief*
- *Colliding with purpose*

May this book help you feel heard, seen, and understood. May my words and the Word of God shared in this book grant you clarity and, most of all, peace.

*I wanted to make my **own** decisions. I didn't want to be told what to do. I did not want to be told what I was going to be. I decided that my life was not going to be robotic. I wanted to explore and discover who I was so that I could determine what would be best for me.*

CHAPTER ONE

THINKING FOR MYSELF

We often believe that we have everything under control because we are making decisions, living life, and doing what we want to do. We don't understand that even in making decisions, we are being influenced by the ideas and opinions of others.

I was born into a beautiful family and a culture where everything was already established. We had few choices but to conform to what was already in place. My father *always* had the last word. Sarcastically, I would tell myself that "father knows best". My father would often say that when we were children, he didn't have a lot of trouble with us because we did what we were told (for the most part). We were mannerable, respectful children that loved and revered our father. He thought for us and directed us in most everything we did. There was no need for a second thought because he had already decided what would be. He had already planned everything; our only job was to do as instructed. Doing as you are told is not necessarily a bad thing, however, as I got older I saw it as confining and controlling. For him, everything was great; for me, not so much. As most children do, I wanted to spread my wings and see what I was capable of doing on my own. In his eyes, everything was working well when I was in compliance because his plans were being fulfilled without question. He often said he didn't have trouble with us until we started to think for ourselves. My dad's desire was that his children have the same values and priorities in life that he had. His focus on God made his perspective bigger than himself. He knew that any problems we would have in life, God could solve if we too, raised our sights to see Him. That was him thinking as a spiritual leader. I was not there yet. His goal was that all of his children would be Christ centered. He wanted the best for me. What was not taken into consideration was the effect his actions were having on me. There were underlying issues being formed that were not immediately evident. When you are not allowed to think for yourself, there is a great possibility that you will begin to experience low self-esteem, low self confidence, feelings of not being good enough, loved or valued for who you are. I don't think my dad understood that I wanted to think for myself, not by myself. What I needed, however, was greater than what I wanted. I needed his life experiences to learn from. I needed him. I needed to be guided by him. I needed him to help me to be an authentic me, not a duplication of him. When parents do not help their children with their authencity, the children will most probably suffer with low self-esteem, fear of judgment of others, and a strong desire to please people. When we are our authentic self, we are more confident in our abilities because we know who we are, what we have to offer, and where we need to improve.

As my siblings and I grew older, we had questions, and when all else failed, "because I said so" would be the response to my questions. As I became intrigued with living life, that response was unacceptable. I was a challenge. I didn't want an effortless "because I said so" answer. I wanted to know when, where, why, and how. I grew up and out in many ways. I knew I was attractive and adventurous. I wanted to make my *own* decisions. I didn't want to be told *what* to do! I did not want to be told *who* I was going to be. I decided that my life was not going to be robotic. I wanted to explore and discover who I was so that I could determine what would be best for me. I wanted to have some say in my present and my future. I was adamant about not being a pastor's wife. Maybe I didn't want to go to church every day of the week. Perhaps I didn't want to grow up and be an evangelist or a missionary. This way of thinking caused people to say that I was rebellious, wayward, disobedient, and even stubborn. All because I did not always follow the beat of my father's drum.

I was not the cookie-cutter "Green Girl." I was often reminded who I was in the third person, "You are Bishop Samuel Green's daughter! You cannot do that!" Well, I set out to prove them all wrong. Sometimes, my friends would introduce me as "Bishop Green's daughter." I felt that I was losing my identity. I thought to myself, "My name is "Naomi Green," not "Bishop Green's daughter"! I wanted to be known for who I was and not for who my parents were. While I acknowledged who my father was, I determined that I would do and be whoever and whatever I wanted to do and be. That was a turning point in my life.

In my mind, thinking for yourself was freedom; freedom to make your own decisions and form your own opinions without depending on others. Having others think for you is not always a bad thing, however, it could be restrictive and leave you feeling manipulated if you accept everything without question. What I came to know was that there is a responsibility that comes with making decisions.

When talking with women about raising their children, my mother would say, "Naomi is going to listen to what I say, but I have to understand that the final decision will always be hers." My father would define that as "planting the seed." When the seed is planted, all that is necessary is nurturing what has been planted. My mother was great at planting and nurturing.

When parents understand that their counsel is only a suggestion toward the final decision, their relationship with their children will grow. That knowledge will open the doors of conversation and you never know what information they will walk away with that will be beneficial to them. Children will think about what was said to them and sometimes your words will linger in their minds as they contemplate their next steps. They may find themselves doing exactly what you have suggested.

Thinking for yourself simply means that your decisions will be well thought out and not spontaneous. Your thoughts are a part of who you are, that's why it is important to find yourself and understand your decisions. As parents, we should allow our children to make decisions. Give them a voice and listen attentively to what they have to say. This enables them to develop responsible decision-making skills early on. It shapes their critical thinking by enlarging their realm of choice. Although you may know what they need, allow them to see it for themselves by thinking it out themselves. Parents should guide their children, instruct them, direct them, and even pick them up should they fall. When children are given the ability to think for themselves, they are empowered. They are better prepared to face real-life challenges that will impact their lives.

Like a child taking their first steps, I wanted and needed support, guidance, and direction. If a child never takes those first steps, they will be carried throughout life, never knowing that they can stand and walk. Taking those first steps will be difficult and the child will fall. When they fall, the loving hands of their parents are what is needed to pick them up and place them on their feet again. No matter how many times they fall, they know that love and support will always be there to pick them up and help them start over again.

I gave my son the same liberty that I desired as a child. After thoroughly discussing his options and its consequences, I allowed him to think for himself and make his own decisions. That door is still open today. This does not mean I no longer have a voice in his life because I do. I am saying that he can talk to me about anything because of the liberty I gave him to think for himself. I encouraged him to think about it, talk about it, and now be about it. Make it happen.

Life is only as good as you make it. Your decisions can make you or break you. Don't live your life fulfilling everyone else's plan for your life or with regret because you did what someone told you to do. **Think for yourself and own it.** Whatever decision you make is yours, no matter who told you to do it. Remember that the consequences are yours just as much as your decisions. No one will live with those consequences but you. I often found myself wanting to point the finger at someone else and play the blame game; "You told me to do this or that, and look at me." No matter who I wanted to blame, it was me that made the active decision to perform an action. I did it. It was *my* decision, my life, and my problem. Likewise, when I made a good decision, the rewards were mine.

My brother, Bishop Dwight Green, told me something that stayed with me all of my life. He said, don't let your past be your present or your present be your future. I was a teenager when he shared those gold nuggets of wisdom with me. At that tender age, I did not understand the value of his words. I was ready to live but I was not prepared for life. I lived long enough to understand what he was saying and it was the best advice he ever gave me. The decisions you make today can decide who you will be tomorrow. The decisions you make today can prevent you from achieving your dreams tomorrow. There is a saying that says, "Don't let your past dictate who you are, but let it be part of who you will become." We don't know what opportunities will arise in our future, but we can prepare for them by making healthy decisions today.

I later understood that my parents were my protectors. As I think about it, they helped me to make some of the best decisions of my life! They wanted to shield me from any type of pain. As a parent, I also wanted to safeguard my son from the storms of life. Every day, I realized that as much as we try, we can't keep pain away from our door. Life happens, and often, with happiness, it brings some pain. That's the balance. Behind every cloud, there is sunshine; it's balance. Allowing me to make decisions responsibly sharpened my critical thinking and self-discipline. Eventually, I was able to make decisions for myself and understand the responsibility that came with my choices. I learned through trial and error, mistakes and mishaps, and gained the ability to make constructive choices about my life and my behavior. I learned that there are consequences and rewards for every action taken and every word spoken. These are life lessons that I will never forget.

As parents, we must remember that we raised our children as best we could, and what we put in them will play out. The apple does not fall far from the tree. Proverbs 22:6 tells us to "train up a child in the way he should go, and when he is old, he will not depart from it." I must say that the Word has played out in my life in many respects. I believe that I am now on the road to becoming the young lady that my parents desired me to be.

In what ways do you need to think for yourself?
Do the opinions of others cause you to question who you really are?

_____

_____

_____

_____

_____

_____

_____

_____

_____

_____

_____

_____

_____

I knew Jesus loved me, but I wanted tangible love from someone I could touch and feel. I wanted love from someone who would love me for <u>me</u>.

CHAPTER TWO

IN PURSUIT OF HAPPINESS

M uch like everyone else, I want to be happy. Being happy is a state of mind, and my state of mind changed *often*. When I was content, I was happy, but when I was sad or lacked fulfillment, I was not. I realized that when I was "happy," I was more positive and focused. I responded to situations differently, and my thought pattern reflected my mental state. With that said, when I was not in my happy place, my thought pattern reflected my mental state, and some bad decisions were made. What I didn't understand was that only **I** could make myself happy.

If I had only taken the unhappy times and chose something positive, I could have projected myself to my happy place. You have heard people say, "Turn that frown upside down" or "Take your lemons and make lemonade." Those statements simply encourage us to find something good, even in the worst situations. When we understand that our happiness is on the inside, we can shift our focus and do something different. Our happiness can be found in what we do or say. No one has a greater influence over you than you. When you tell yourself to be happy, your emotions will comply.

Sometimes friends and family think they know what will make you happy, but I found that not to be true. I looked for happiness in many ways and thought I found it; each time, my faux happiness was short-lived. In my happiness pursuit, I discovered that what makes me happy is not necessarily what makes everyone else happy. I thought that love would make me happy, so I searched for it. My dad said that I could find it in Jesus Christ, but that was not what I was looking for at that time. I knew Jesus loved me, but I wanted tangible love from someone I could touch and feel. I wanted love from someone who would love me for **me.** My journey opened my eyes to the fact that I did not know what I wanted because I did not know who I was. How could I ask someone to love me for me when I didn't love me? I didn't even know who I was. My first love should have been me. I should have taken the time as a young person to identify who I was and love myself. I didn't understand many things that I did or tendencies that I had because I failed to take the time to study myself, to know myself. It takes time to get to know yourself and you are worth the time.

Have you ever heard the saying *"looking for love in all the wrong places,"* that was me! I wore my heart on my sleeve, and it was trampled. I fell into relationships that were not good for me and where I wanted to go in life. I attracted the wrong men into my life. They could see that I lacked something; some of them took advantage of my weakened state of mind, while other men saw my lack of confidence and took me as an easy target. Needless to say, I made countless bad choices before realizing what would be good for me.

In my search for happiness, I did *whatever* I thought necessary to fit in. I wanted to belong to someone and often found myself in places I would not have been in a more positive state of mind. When I was in my best place, I knew how to say NO, but when I was not, my thoughts were scattered, and I was quite vulnerable. My feelings about myself were all up in the air. When I was in my best place, there was nothing I could not do, places I could go, or what I could be. When I was not in my best place, I didn't think I was good enough and questioned every decision I made. I found myself being a people pleaser. My self-esteem was constantly under attack.

I was in love three times in my life. Those relationships took a lot of time and effort. I learned that love is a high that I never wanted to come down from. I also learned that real love takes a lot of work from both parties and can sometimes hurt. When I fell in love for the first time, I was a church girl, but I did not have a real relationship with God. I was not seeking it, but **it happened**. I was in love, for real, for the first time! I was overcome with love for him to the point that I told God I would get saved if He allowed me to marry this man. After experiencing so much hurt in my life, I just wanted God to let me be happy this one time! When you are hurt, it's not easy to wish yourself happy, so I went to God, the One that does all things well, and asked Him to let me have this one, PLEASE! The problem with that request is that God wanted me to love

Him for Him and not for what He could do for me. Just like me! He wants what I want: **to be loved.**

We often bargain with God, and when He doesn't answer the way we want, we get upset. I learned that my natural desires should never motivate me to pray to God. So, we can all agree that my request was way out of line. Needless to say, the relationship did not turn out the way I anticipated. God's answer was not what I thought it would be. I was angry with God and the world. I set out to live my life, not caring what anyone thought. Not thinking about the outcome of my actions, this mindset landed me single and pregnant.

There was one night that changed my life forever. I was in an unexpected place, experiencing something that I never thought would happen to me. This resulted in me having a child with a man who wanted nothing to do with us. The degradation that I felt was overwhelming. What happens to you due to your decisions is yours to own. I found myself in a place I never imagined, and neither was I prepared for.

I raised my son with the guidance of my parents and family. Feeling that I let myself down again, I wanted to pick myself up and start again. I worked hard every day as I had additional responsibility as the provider for my son. I greatly appreciate my parents for not turning their back on me. I had forsaken everything that they had taught me, but they were always there for me. They did not walk away from me but instead walked with me on this journey. I desperately needed them and am glad they did not leave me alone. My dad once told me it was meant for my son, Nathaniel, to be here, just not how I brought him here. **I'll take that.** He had the most unique way of voicing his truth. I miss my parents in ways I can never fully express.

After several years of adventure and experimenting with life, I experienced love again. I allowed myself to be involved in a relationship like none other that I had before. It was different and fascinating. I was caught up and fought anyone who said it didn't make sense. When I look back at it, **none of it made sense.** I was in such dire need of affection that I was blind to the signs when they were right before me. I wanted to see where it would go, and unfortunately, it was limited, filled with obstacles, and then it was over. We are not always ready for who we allow ourselves to love. I loved him and believe he loved me, but he was not the one for me. No matter how much I ran from the truth, it became apparent when he got married and moved away. Another lesson learned.

> *"Keep your heart with all diligence, for*
> *out of it are the issues of life."*
> *—Proverbs 4:23*

I was later introduced to my husband, a man I had watched give his life to the Lord over 30 years prior. When he joined the church, I quickly realized that he was **not** my type because he was deeply saved and into soul-winning. I just was not there yet, so I didn't look at him twice. He married a friend of mine and they raised their family in the church. After 25 years of marriage, his wife passed. I remember this was difficult for him and their adult children. I was working in ministry at my home church and had stopped looking for love. I was dedicated to caring for my mom and working with my dad in ministry. While attending the National Convocation in Memphis, Tennessee, with thousands of the saints, my roommate said to me, "Have you seen Elder Ward?"

"No, I have not," was my response.

From that time on, our paths continued to cross. His daughter asked me to contact him from time to time because he was now alone. When I first entered this relationship, I was a friend who comforted him in his loss. I would call and check on him and talk about his wife, my friend. My dad said that something will happen if you talk to someone too long, and again, he was right. We realized that our feelings were growing from casual conversation to an attraction.

When love entered my heart the third time, I said yes. The third time was a charm. To say it was a charm may be glamourizing it just a little bit. For me, love has always been a challenge – searching for it and finding it. This time, I didn't have to find love; love found me.

I had often heard my father say to the congregation, "Marriage is an institution. You can lose your mind." While I have found that to be true, I also found that the Bible is right. 1 Peter 4:8 says, "Above all, love each other deeply, because love covers over a multitude of sins" (ESV). I understand better why God told us to love our neighbor as ourselves. He issued that command because hatred stirs conflict, but love covers all. I am not perfect, and neither is my husband, but we love each other. In loving each other, we are committed to cover each other and to forgive each other. We have committed to making our relationship work, and I make that commitment daily. I reflect the love that God has for me by loving and being ready to forgive my husband. I want to be clear that forgiving and covering your mate doesn't mean standing idly by and allowing yourself to be taken for granted or disrespected. If something needs to be addressed, there is a way to do that. Distinguish between what can be overlooked and what needs to be addressed. By all means, do not walk around with hurt in your heart because something has been done to you by your spouse. Have a conversation and come to an understanding. Encourage, build, and pray for each other. Keep God as the center of your relationship.

In your pursuit of happiness, first, find out who you are, then you can identify what will make you happy, and the gateway to happiness will open. When I discovered who I was and learned to love myself, I became a candidate to love someone else. When you are introduced to yourself, your authentic self, you will want to do what is necessary to make yourself happy before aspiring to bring happiness to others. When you are happy, it flows to everyone you come in contact with.

Do you know what truly makes you happy?
Are you searching for love or waiting for love to find you?

_____

_____

_____

_____

_____

_____

_____

_____

_____

_____

_____

_____

_____

_____

_____

*Love is patient and kind; love does not envy or boast;
it is not arrogant [5] or rude. It does not insist on its
own way; it is not irritable or resentful,[b] [6] it does
not rejoice at wrongdoing, but rejoices with
the truth. [7] Love bears all things, believes all
things, hopes all things, endures all things.*
—I Corinthians 13:4-7

My father preached a provocative gospel and would use me as an example often in an effort to provoke me to accept Jesus Christ. My response to his provocation was rebellion.

CHAPTER THREE

MY FATHER WAS MY PASTOR

I was born and raised in the Christian church. I was a student of Sunday School, Young People Willing Worker (YPWW), Purity Class, and Vacation Bible School. Being raised in the church, I learned many valuable life lessons. I learned to respect my parents and my elders. I learned to reverence the altar and God's Holy sacraments. I was taught to pray and read the Bible. Most importantly, I was taught to love God and His people.

In addition to attending church on Tuesday, Friday, and Sunday, my father would teach us Bible scriptures in his free time at home. Some people may think that is a little over the top, but he wanted to be sure that we knew God and His Word. He desired to please God in everything that he did and raised us to do the same. When church conventions came around, or additional church services were scheduled, we were front and center. I have heard other preachers' children say that they were dragged to church. That was not our story. We enjoyed going to church. It was almost our second home.

My relationship with my Father was loving. We were both strong-willed and could be stubborn, but our emotion toward each other was nothing but love. We were playfully affectionate, and he knew when I was around because I was always doing something to him. Our conversations were deep and honest. When he talked, there was very little gray area. I guess that's where I get it from. He was politically correct and concise. He could get right to the point! He was a man of the Bible. He did not play when it came to God.

My dad was a soul winner. He knew how to present Christ to you. He was creative, motivational, charismatic, and inspiring. I love him! Imagine my surprise when, after all of this "God" that surrounded me, I found myself pregnant and unmarried. Now, this was not an immaculate conception, so I wasn't surprised altogether. I did the deed but was not prepared when the doctor told me that I was going to be a mother. The reality hit me *real* hard, *real* fast. My parents were not going to be happy about this news! Everyone who knew my dad knew that he was about pleasing God and hard on sin. The situation that I found myself in was a difficult one.

I was not only the pastor's daughter, but the pastor is Bishop Samuel L. Green, Jr.! My father preached a provocative gospel and would use me as an example often in an effort to provoke me to accept Jesus Christ. My response to his provocation was rebellion. I was determined to do things **my** way, no matter what. My rebellion led me right to this place.

When it was noised abroad that I was with child, everyone wanted to know my dad's response. My parents were disappointed. I think that made me feel worse than the act itself. Church people waited to see how my dad would handle the situation. I did not want him to be any more uncomfortable than he already was, so I removed myself from all positions in the church, including the choir. I took the expected steps, begged the church's pardon for my sin, and sat myself down. That was the proper way at the time. To say the least, things have changed! After talking to my parents, I made an appointment to talk to my pastor. Yes, I said my pastor. I know my pastor was also my father, but I needed my pastor.

I went to my pastor's office, and he listened to me, consoled me, and counseled me. He advised that he has always preached against sin and will continue to do so. He wanted me to know that when these subjects come up, he's not preaching about me; he's preaching against sin, and there is a difference. When my son's father refused to step up, my father was an excellent example of fatherhood. He didn't change anything to cushion my landing, which was good for me. My mother supported me by helping me not to make the same mistake again and being the strength I needed to be the mother I should be for my son. They were my rock!

My son was not a mistake, but I own the fact that I could have made a better choice. Not only did I disappoint my parents, I hurt God's heart. While I intended to live life on my terms, I ended up bringing a life into the world. My son, Nathaniel, has helped me grow, mature, and own my choices. We have all fallen short of God's grace, but you can bounce back, just like I did.

In what ways have you bounced back from your poor choices?

"For all have sinned, and come short of the glory of God; Being justified freely by his grace through the redemption that is in Christ Jesus: Whom God hath set forth to be a propitiation through faith in his blood, to declare his righteousness for the remission of sins that are past, through the forbearance of God; To declare, I say, at this time his righteousness: that he might be just, and the justifier of him which believeth in Jesus."
—Romans 3:23-26 KJV

CHAPTER FOUR

NOT THE BLACK SHEEP, JUST DIFFERENT

S ociety tells us that every person in the family has an identity. The oldest is deemed the one with the most responsibility and will probably fill the role of surrogate parent. The middle children are often described as diplomatic and adaptable often popular and patient. And well, we all can describe the baby. The youngest gets all the attention and usually gets their own way. In my family, some of this is true some of the time. I say that because we don't fit into a mold. We were brought up to be individuals. So how am I the black sheep and not just an individual that is different from the others? Who said I couldn't be different? I don't fit in the box so I have to be the black sheep? NO!! I refused to accept that.

As a young person, I can remember being told that I was different. I took that as a compliment. When I didn't fit in I was told that I was the black sheep. That took on a very different meaning for me. Yes, I will agree that I am different.

I worked at being different. I didn't want to be like everybody else. I wanted to stand out in a crowd and I still do. That was a far cry from being the black sheep. The black sheep was not anything that I wanted to be associated with. The black sheep of the family is rebellious, misunderstood and just didn't fit. Okay, maybe I was all three but still not the black sheep. The term "black sheep" carries negative connotations. I didn't want to be considered in a dark light, but sure shooting, very little good was said about me. You either liked me or you didn't. Some didn't like me and could not tell me why. That's their problem and their loss.

Some may disagree but I was often the subject of conversation. I am not making myself larger than life, but I do know that preachers' children are always judged more harshly than anyone else in the church. That was it. The preacher's family is the example for everything. It's difficult to live in that box. Too often even your good is evil spoken of. More times than not, the good that I did was overshadowed by my wrongdoing. I remember defending myself over and over again, to no avail. I had to realize that people were going to believe what they want to believe. I decided that just because they said it didn't mean it was me. I know it may have been hard to believe at the time, but I loved my parents and looked up to them and the example that they were. I still love them. It was nothing to come to church and feel like I was the subject of the sermon for the day. He could be talking about anything and when his eyes fell on me, immediately the subject turned to me. I didn't want to think it true, but some people were entertained by my misfortune. Some agreed with my dad as he talked about my life of sin, and though he was right, that technique was not winning me to a Christian lifestyle. Looking back at it, he may not have been talking about me. Maybe he was talking about sin and because I was a sinner, the sermon found me. GUILTY AS SIN. My father preached a provocative message and many thought it had no effect on me. I got to a place where I almost gave up on myself. That day, I mustered the courage to agree with what others were saying about me. "I will own it. I am the black sheep!" I lost my fight. They were saying it so okay, here it is. I thought I did not fit in, even with my own family. My siblings were all men and women of the gospel, and I was not. I will even take it a step further to say that in my mind, I was so far removed from what they all stood for that I wondered why did God birth me to this family. I was odd man out! This can't be my life! What I soon found out was that the altar was the only place that I fit in. Everyone that was there was in the fight of their life, just like me.

In an effort to understand myself, I went to therapy. Yes, I carried myself to a therapist to get the help that I so desperately needed. I was extending my hands for help. I volunteered to get the help I needed because I realized that this life was not the life that I wanted. It was not the life that I was supposed to have. I paid for the therapeutic help and kept every appointment. I sincerely wanted to understand what was happening to me. Why was I spiraling out of control like this? I couldn't blame all of this on the devil because whatever he did through me, it was because I allowed it. I knew this was out of character for me, so there was a negative force that I had given myself to that was encouraging this damaging lifestyle. In scripture, I found John 10:10 speaking to me, "The thief cometh not, but for to steal, and to kill, and to destroy." That's where I was, living a life of destruction. No future but death. I was looking forward to my last appointment with the doctor, for her to help me get to the root of the problem and how to end all of this. I would finally receive the answers that I so desired. When I had my final appointment, I expected a written report from the doctor. I was, instead informed that someone that worked in the system (from my father's office) had picked up the report. When I got home, my dad had read the report and was not happy with what it said. I can't imagine that the person that delivered that report to my dad had me in mind at all. They had gotten brownie points at my expense. That was my business and needless to say, though the services rendered were necessary and helpful, I did not go to her office again. I felt that my confidential information was no longer confidential. I felt betrayed. This action was supposed to close whatever door that had been opened to help me find deliverance. I was down but I was not out. I gathered every bit of fight I had left and fought for myself.

Time can heal deep wounds, if you let it. My father and I would have deep conversations. Sometimes about me. Sometimes about life. Sometimes about God. One day we were talking and I took the opportunity to speak from my heart. I thought I was the worst child my parents had and told him so. I knew he was listening and I poured it all out for him to hear. He assured me that that couldn't be farther from the truth. This is one of three conversations I remember that I had with him that reached me. He shared with me what he saw in me. He told me how strong I am. He acknowledged the call of God on my life. He told me everything that a young woman needs to hear from her father. Finally, I knew he saw me for me and not a black sheep.

We are all uncomfortable with being the topic of discussion to the point that we want to know what is being said. Scripture reveals that even Jesus asked His disciples, "Who do people say the Son of Man is?" They replied, "Some say John the Baptist; others say Elijah; and still others, Jeremiah or one of the prophets." "But what about you?" he asked. "Who do you say I am?" Simon Peter answered, "You are the Messiah, the Son of the living God." Jesus replied, "Blessed are you, Simon son of Jonah, for this was not revealed to you by flesh and blood, but by my Father in heaven. And I tell you that you are Peter,[a] and on this rock I will build my church, and the gates of Hades[b] will not overcome it. I will give you the keys of the kingdom of heaven; whatever you bind on earth will be[c] bound in heaven, and whatever you loose on earth will be[d] loosed in heaven." (Matthew 16:13-19)

The importance of this scripture to me is that the people that lived with Him could identify Who He is. Not only that but Jesus knew them as well. I am so sure that Peter was walking on air after that conversation. When my father poured into me, it meant all of the world to me. No matter what anyone else thought, I knew what my father thought about me and how he felt toward me. I could be different. I can be who God has called me to be. All of the provocation in the world was not able to do for me what was done for me in that one conversation. He was listening, and so was I. The time was right.

I share this to the herd of black sheep that are trying to fit in. You probably won't fit. I want you to believe in yourself.

God did not make us all the same. He made us in His image and there are so many facets to God. Seek to know His ways. Seek to know Him and by so doing, you will get to know yourself. My husband has often said that we should seek to understand others. I agree. We spend a lot of time wanting to be understood but very little time seeking to understand others. If we were to try to understand others, we would remove the labels that we have placed on them and reach out our hands to help them. We would take our mouths off of them and say a prayer for them. People are sometimes misdirected as they search for who they are. Let's find something positive to say to them. Something positive to say about them. Let's build them up instead of tearing them down.

I am different. I am who God says I am. I am seeking His will for me. That's what God loves.

I obeyed my parents as much as possible when they instructed us to love and respect the saints, but I did not like it at all! The hypocrisy caused me to turn my back on the church.

CHAPTER FIVE

TIME FOR A CHANGE

I have often heard that there is nothing new under the sun and found this to be true. Life is a cycle, just one big circle. We watch caterpillars go through their life cycle as they blossom into a beautiful butterfly. Likewise, we go through cycles of life from fetus to baby, to child, then adolescent to adult, and finally you are a senior. Everything is cyclical, meaning, to every beginning, there is an end. Seasons change. As we go from day to day, year to year, we go through physical changes that allow us to reach adulthood, and hopefully, we are wiser because of our experiences.

My life was a vicious cycle of rebellion, repentance, grace, and asking for mercy. I spent many years running behind my selfish desires that got me nowhere. I started to feel like the hamster on a wheel, running and winding up in the same place. No progress, no joy, no peace; just tired and empty. With all that I did in the world, church remained a constant. I was there, not on time, sometimes inactive, but there, nonetheless. Bishop Samuel Green always said, "If you are sitting in the sanctuary, I can plant the seed." The Bible says that all flesh will know who God is. Bishop made sure that we knew who God was and planted seeds in us, hoping we would turn from our wicked ways. For me, the seed being planted was removing every excuse of me not wanting to know Him.

Having been born in the church, I had seen God do great things for others, but I had also seen some ugly things done by church people to my parents and others. I obeyed my parents as much as possible when they instructed us to love and respect the saints, but I did not like it at all! The hypocrisy caused me to turn my back on the church. I didn't want that part of it. I told my dad that I did not see the need to accept Christ if I was going to continue doing what I was doing in the world. I did not want to be a hypocrite. I wanted Christ but not the hypocrisy that I saw in the church.

I continued to sing in the choir and be active in the church while still being active in the world. Remember now, the scripture explains that a double-minded man shall receive nothing from the Lord. There I was though. When my flesh called, I answered. I enjoyed the activities at church. Bishop Green had a heart for young people, so there was always something for us to do. Our church was one of the first church choirs with a band, and we were jamming every time we came to church! It was a good time.

I knew I was empty because when I would come to church, God's Word would find me and lift me to the altar of repentance. My heart was filled with God on Sunday, but because I had not made a commitment, I was right back to my old self by Wednesday. I realized that I didn't have what I needed to make the change stick. With that said, I can vividly remember a revival at St. John COGIC. The evangelist was Paul Reed. He delivered the gospel in a way that spoke to me. During the revival, my Dad said, "I want to see my daughter roll down these aisles under the power of the Holy Ghost." My first thought was prideful because I might fall out on the floor, *but why do I have to roll up and down the aisle?* Nope, I already decided that if I had the Holy Ghost experience, I was **not** rolling on the floor!

The revival was a success, so Bishop extended it. Usually, when I went to church, I would sit with my friends, and we would cut up, **but not this time**. Every night, I sat on the front row with my Bible, waiting for the Word of God to change my life. I was tired of running. I was persistent in seeking Him, and God did not disappoint me. I remember standing at the front of the church, praising God with everyone else. Suddenly, my language changed, and I began to speak in the heavenly language. It was an experience I had never had in my life. I was baptized in the Holy Ghost! I was so excited that when I could, I wanted to tell someone I felt would understand my feelings. The service was coming to a close, and I went to my mother's office and said, "Mom, I just received the Baptism of the Holy Ghost!" She calmly replied, "That's nice." Albeit I was a little surprised at her response, I was on cloud nine! Couldn't nobody tell me nothing. I received the Holy Ghost, and my life was going to be different.

That was an incredible experience, but I didn't expect that now that I was baptized, I had to grow spiritually in the Lord. Growing spiritually required maturity and denying my flesh. That part of my journey was difficult. There were many in the Bible that walked with God daily and had a relationship with

Him but still had to deal with their demons. David's demons caused him to commit adultery and murder. Judas' demons caused him to betray Christ and commit suicide. Peter's demons caused him to curse and cut the soldier's ear off. To see Jesus's disciples struggle with their proclivities taught me that no matter how close you are to God in your mind, you'd better know that as long as you exist on this earth, keep your eye on the devil and keep your flesh in check. Galatians 5:16 tells us to walk in the Spirit and not after the flesh. According to Romans 8:13, it is necessary to mortify the deeds of the flesh regularly.

I often heard that there is one baptism in Holy Ghost, but there are many refillings. I didn't understand that, but after further study, I found that being filled with Holy Spirit is a recurring event. Being baptized in the Holy Spirit was my initial experience, but we are constantly encouraged by scripture to be continually filled with Holy Spirit (the power), which is a daily practice. Being in the presence of Holy Ghost (the person) daily basking in His presence.

Not focusing on the fact that I had to build upon my initial experience with Holy Spirit, I kept tempting God. I found myself not seeking God as fervently as I once did. My eyes were no longer toward God, but toward what I wanted. Like we do in a natural relationship, I became relaxed with God and began to do some of the things that I used to do.

Natural relationship tip: appreciate your mate, pay attention to your mate, love your mate, and when you need your mate, they will be there for you

While I was relaxing, I was becoming spiritually weak. I can remember the sayig that seven days without prayer makes one weak. That described me in a nutshell. The desire to do what was right was now overpowered by my weaknesses. It appeared that I had very little spiritual strength. When I would do good, evil was present. Romans 7:17-25 explains that there was a war going on inside me. I knew what was right to do, but I lacked the power to do it. The power of sin within kept setting me up to fail, interrupting my good intentions. I kept falling and needed help. Something had happened while I was in spiritual slumber that caused me to fail every time I tried to do what I believed God intended for me to do. I was at the end of my rope and was reaching for help. I found myself spiritually empty because I had not nurtured my spirit man. I had catered to my flesh and given myself everything I desired, and now, in my sinful state, I felt like I was calling God, and even He had turned His back on me. Truth be told, He had not turned His back on me. I had turned my back on Him.

I traveled to the Church of God in Christ's National Auxiliaries in Ministry Convention and attended the youth service. The speaker had a great gift. I sat in the service, and at a certain point in ministry, he left the pulpit and walked out into the conference center where people were congregating and socializing, with the microphone, still preaching, illustrating that we are to go everywhere and preach the gospel. When the call to discipleship was made, I found myself on the altar, with many others, crying out to God. It was in that service that my relationship with Holy Ghost was restored, with the evidence of speaking in tongues. Because I experienced it, I *know* that there are many re-fillings. This experience was nothing like the initial experience, but I was so happy for the presence of Holy Spirit in my life again.

God had not turned His back on me, but I had to find my way back to Him, and that was a process. My life was filled with contradictions where I wanted to serve God with all my heart and mind but was pulled by the influence of sin to do something entirely different. That which I had nurtured had the stronger power over me. The lust of the flesh was stronger because I always gave in to it. Lesson learned. I now have a time set for scripture study and prayer. During those times, I can commune with God, and in His presence, **I am filled with Holy Spirit.**

What changes do you need to make to live a life on purpose? What cycles do you need to break to live purpose-driven life? Have you been filled since you first believed?

_____

_____

_____

_____

_____

_____

_____

_____

_____

_____

_____

_____

_____

"And they were all filled with the Holy Spirit and began to speak with other tongues, as the Spirit was giving them utterance."
—Acts 2:4

Life as I knew it had completely changed, and returning to my norm was impossible. The people that complete me were gone. My world was collapsing!

CHAPTER SIX

UNTIL IT HAPPENED

I t is funny how grief slips up on you and changes your entire life. Yes, funny, but not funny. I was very young when my paternal grandfather died, but I remember when my maternal grandfather died. We were in California at one of the COGIC National Summer Conventions. I remember my father calling us to his room to deliver this devastating news. I could not believe what I was hearing. Life as I knew it had changed with his words. Big Daddy was gone. Many years later, my remaining grandparents passed.

My experience with death is that it always allowed me time to recover and breathe. When death took a loved one, I had ten to twenty years to adjust to the absence of my loved one. That was *my* norm. There was a significant lapse between the death and mourning. I never gave a great deal of thought to the grief and loss of close loved ones when I was younger. After the passing of my grandparents, the grief of loss was far from my mind. I stopped thinking about further loss. I even went so far as never thinking about living life without my parents, siblings, or extended family. It was a given that they would always be here, praying for me, supporting and encouraging me. Life without them was not even a thought . . . **until it happened.**

My mother's passing in 2007 seemed to break the family chain, which was never repaired. Her demise caused me to accept that death is a part of life. Eight years later, my father departed, and then, within six years of his passing, I was surprised at the death of my niece, my sister, and my brother. All of these losses were traumatic and completely unexpected. I felt as if my entire inner circle was diminishing. Life as I knew it had taken a drastic dip, and returning to my norm was impossible. The people that complete me were gone. My world was collapsing!

My family is very close. Like other families, we have our dysfunction, but we love each other. Losing a family member is not like losing a friend or co-worker. Losing a family member is similar to an amputation. It is like losing a limb. The *thought* of that limb not being there does not compare to the *reality* that it is no longer there. Although I am not an amputee, many people who've had an amputation experience grief, depression, anxiety, and bereavement, similar to experiencing the loss of a loved one. The expectancy of your family member returning from a long trip, walking in the door at any time from work or shopping, is similar to the loss of sensation from your amputated limb. Out of habit, an amputee will reach out for their limb as a grieving person reaches out for their loved one. I have picked up my phone to call my mom, only to remind myself that she is out of my grasp. I have had a question about something I was reading and wanted to call my brother, but he is no longer available. Experiencing the warmth of my niece's smile and laughter was no longer an option. The desire to visit my sister and my father for hours is still there but unrequited. Constant reminders that they are no longer here are an everyday occurrence. Granted, the loss of a limb differs from the loss of a family member, but the emotional response is eerily similar.

Although I grieved the death of all of my family members, the experience of my parents' death was far different from the death of my siblings. I am not sure why, but it was vastly different. It has often been said that no parent should have to bury a child; therefore, we live expecting to bury our parents, but not preparing for it at all.

I never had a <u>single</u> thought of burying my siblings. The emotion I faced at my parents' demise was very different from my siblings. I could wrap my head around my parents going on to be with the Lord. I can't say I was prepared, but I could understand it. When we face grief, we must realize it will impact us differently based on our relationship with the person. Losing my parents was hard, but losing my siblings seems almost unfathomable. Yes, I was close to my parents, but there were activities that I went through in life that I did not share with them. My parents were my disciplinarians and my advisors, but I did not share certain things with them. My brothers and sisters were my sounding board. I vented to them. My parents were my support and I needed them. My siblings are my support and I celebrate with them. My parents did not share their faults or problems with me. My siblings shared everything, and I cried with them, and they with me.

While all of my siblings are necessary in my life, I bonded with them differently.

In a moment, death entered and changed my entire life. The departure of my family members was all managed differently as well. My siblings' death was unexpected, and to function, I had to isolate the feelings of loss that I felt. Some days, I was completely numb. Every day, I was prayerful that God would be my strength.

Thankfully, my parents did not have to bury their children but siblings burying siblings, oh my! Receiving the unexpected call that your sibling has passed is an occurrence that takes your breath away. Making the phone call to inquire about the status of your sibling is antagonizing. You expect them to answer and have a conversation, but you don't hear their voice on the other end of the phone. I came to the understanding, eventually, that yes, my sibling has passed, but they have a whole family that should be considered. Their spouse and children are grieving, too. **What do you say? How do you act?** We are always there for each other, suffering silently. Our extended family is suffering as well. Inwardly we are torn to pieces but outwardly we are strong for each other. The death of my siblings threw me for a loop (sometimes, I am still loopy). God has been my strength.

I suggest to anyone who has lost a loved one. Give yourself permission to experience *every* emotion. Allow yourself to grieve and heal. This is not to say to be out of control or act out, but let's be mature. Grieve and heal. Some may say, "Get over it". Well, let me say, I am not 'over it' and don't expect to be any time soon. I am, however, healing and dealing with my losses. Sometimes, I am sad. Some days, I am angry. On other days, I am simply numb. Cherished memories have sometimes put a smile on my face. Whatever the emotion, I give myself permission to lean in, remembering the blessing of their life that God gave to me.

How have you dealt with your grief and loss?
What things can you do better to help yourself grieve in a healthier way?

_____

_____

_____

_____

_____

_____

_____

_____

_____

_____

_____

_____

_____

_____

"Surely he hath borne our griefs,
and carried our sorrows…"
—Isaiah 53:4

I cannot be contained; therefore, I do not fit in a box.

CHAPTER SEVEN

WHO IS NAOMI IN HER OWN WORDS?

My mother always told us to be the best person we could be. She encouraged me that no one could do a better job at being Naomi Green than Naomi Green. So, what does that mean? Who in the world is Naomi? **I did not know**. I spent the greater part of my life answering that question. I have had to find out who I am, what I like, what I want to do, where I want to go, and how I think. These questions and more are necessary because there are so many facets to who we are. I've discovered that there are so many parts to me being me.

I am not the person today that I was thirty years ago. Life experiences have caused new pieces of me to emerge. While some things have changed, some things have remained the same.

I've always loved life! I love living life! I love making life happen! I am a lot of fun and love to laugh, but I can be *very* serious. I love a good time, but I also need my quiet time.

I love to learn new things. I love to travel. I love God and have *learned* how to love His people. I cannot be contained; therefore, I do not fit in a box. I am creative, have big dreams, and do not give up easily. I want what I want, when I want it! I am an abundance of a woman. I am unapologetically ME!

Looking at everything I love is like looking at my resume. Nothing is like the last thing. I love the challenge. I love the adventure. I love the experience. There have been times when I have second-guessed myself. At those times, God has placed people in my life who push me forward and tell me that it is possible, doable, and I can do it! My secret was embracing who I could be tomorrow beyond who I am today. To do that, I had to push myself daily to be better, to do better.

I must say that my parents were right. . . about everything. Had I listened to them and gained from their knowledge, my life would have been so different. But, maybe I would not be the strong individual that stands before you today. I realize that my words may be dismissed by some readers, but it is available for everyone that picks up this book. My parents shared with me truth and consequences and lots of times, I chose the consequences. I believe the Word of God came alive in my life often. In particular, Romans 8:28 comforted me numerous times when it said "And we know that all things work together for good to them that love God, to them who are the called according to his purpose". I am filled with His purpose.

Every job I have worked has been different and had a purpose for me to become the woman I am today. I believe that I also served a purpose in each of my places of employment. It could have been something as small as a smile, a kind word, or even a word of prayer for a co-worker; even my tenure had a purpose. I am growing every day and becoming who I was created to be.

As a young adult, I was introduced to business and administration. I learned how to work with people. I learned to help others and to recognize the importance of it. I learned to work independently and as a team to get the job done. All of this is important for where I am now, a place I never desired to be, the wife of a pastor.

All of these abilities are necessary for the life of the pastor's wife. In this role, I must be innovative, authoritative, loving, understanding, supportive, resourceful, and, most importantly, understand my assignment. While getting to know myself on a deeper level, I found that I am fearfully and wonderfully made, and I needed to spread that message to those in my sphere of influence. I have channeled my creativity into a weekly Facebook Live broadcast. Over the years, the limits that hover over my life are gradually melting away.

We shortchange ourselves and keep the world from experiencing the brilliance of who we are. If you are not willing to stretch yourself to uncomfortable places, you will not be able to be the example that so many people need in this world.

Defining who I am is an ongoing process. I am still learning who I am because if I allow myself to, I can find something new about me every day. What has not changed is that I live out loud, laugh heartily, and love with my whole heart.

Describe yourself in your own words.
What do you wish people understood about you?

_____

_____

_____

_____

_____

_____

_____

_____

_____

_____

_____

_____

_____

_____

_____

"I will praise thee; for I am fearfully and wonderfully made: marvelous are thy works; and that my soul knoweth right well."
—Psalm 139:14

CHAPTER EIGHT

SMILING THROUGH
THE TEARS

In conclusion, I have been transparent about my life experiences. This book is a testimony of the goodness of God. I have shared my experiences and knowledge I gained from those experiences in hopes of helping someone. God gave me kind, loving parents. He placed me in a family that cared for me. Sometimes I didn't understand, but the more I pushed, the more they pulled. I have to say that even in my darkest moments, when it looked like I would never get it, my parents and siblings were there. They were there to let me know that everything would be alright. Everyone needs a good support system. So many times they pulled me through. Yes, there were some hard times. Yes, I cried many days and nights. The answers that I needed sometimes came through my tears. It was when I didn't see how things were going to play out. I was at my wits end. No where to go, not knowing who to call. With my back against the wall, I cried dealing with the hurt and pain from decisions I had made. I cried in disappointment when reality slapped me in my face. I cried when my emotions were all out of whack. I cried when I couldn't keep it together. I couldn't keep living like this. I cried! I learned how to smile through my tears. I could be hurting on the inside, but I was somehow able to laugh with others. Broken and shattered, beyond the tears, I smile.

Then one day, I turned to God and gave it all to Him. I gave up fighting against all that I knew I needed. I gave up to God. My dad always said, we are running away from what we should be filled up with. Sometimes we need to just stop. Just stop defending our stance long enough to hear God. Just stop talking long enough to hear His voice. Just stop being so busy that we don't see God at work. Stop being a big shot long enough to know that God is greater. Stop thinking that you have it all together when everything around you is tumbling down. Just stop! "For the Lord gives wisdom; from his mouth come knowledge and understanding" (Proverbs 9:10). When I stopped running, God showed me how to praise Him inspite of what I went through. He taught me how to "dance in the rain". He pulled the pieces of my shattered life together. I learned to give God praise in the midst of it all. I got really good at "dancing in the rain". Yes, I still had unanswered questions. But when I look back over everything that I have endured, God has been good to me. He didn't give up on me nor did He let me give up. The storms kept raging, but God has shown me to cry out to Him and He will answer and show me great and mighty things that I can't even fathom. I don't have to worry because He is the peace giver. He is my comfort. He has taught me to cast my cares upon Him because He cares for me. As the songwriter said, "When I think of the goodness of Jesus, and what he has done for me, my soul cries out, "Hallelujah!" I praise God for saving me". So many scriptures and songs come to my mind right now. Songs that carried me through the lonely nights. The nights that I thought that I was left alone to walk this journey, only to find out that God was carrying me all of the time. I didn't do this alone. It was all God!

I finally got it! Through every one of my situations, I have learned. So, here I am, full circle, believing God. God is so good! Life experiences did not kill me but made me stronger. I have learned that there is no problem that God cannot solve. I have learned that everything that I need is in Him. I have learned to trust in God. I have learned that without Him I can do nothing. I have learned that every good gift comes from God. I have learned that Jesus is my help, a very present help. I have learned that when I talk to Him, He hears, He understands, and He answers. I have learned that He is a burden bearer. I have learned that no one ever cared for me like Jesus. I have learned that I can depend on Him to catch me when I am falling. Through it all, I have learned. That is so important. Just like my parents taught me why something was wrong, God helped me to obtain a knowledge of sin, what it will do to you, and its consequences, by allowing me to have these life experiences that I so desperately desired. My dad told me that I didn't have to experience certain things, but I was bound and determined that yes I did. He was right, again! I learned by the experiences I suffered through. I have heard that experience is the best teacher but that is not true for everyone. If a person is no smarter from what they've experienced, seen, and heard, all of it was for naught. Experience alone is no guarantee of a learning opportunity. For my experiences to be a learning opportunity, I had to change the way that I thought about my experiences. I had to see them as a chance to learn; learn what not to do again. My life is filled with lessons. Some lessons I had to go through over and over again, but I learned nonetheless. It's insanity to keep doing the same thing over and over again, expecting a different outcome. The result of my life lessons is that they helped me improve and make better decisions for my future.

I have often been reminded of past sins, bad decisions, and yes, life experiences. In those times, I am thankful that I am not there anymore. My life has taught me many lessons about myself and God. That is my testimony! Life has taught me that knowledge is power. I am thankful that God's love has lifted me from the bonds of sin, despair, and doubt. Every opportunity that I have, I share my testimony to those that will listen and apply the knowledge that I have gained so that I can continually improve myself and the lives of others. Through it all I have learned to trust in God and His Word. Everyday, God's Word frees me, heals me, improves me, strengthens me, restores me, and makes me right. God is so good and He loves me, inspite of me. For that reason, I love Him!

I am courageous. I choose courage over comfort. In spite of my fears, I am courageous.

_____

"Be strong and courageous. Do not be afraid or terrified because of them, for the Lord your God goes with you; he will never leave you nor forsake you."
Deuteronomy 31:6

_____

_____

_____

_____

_____

_____

_____

_____

_____

_____

_____

_____

I am brave and bold in my pursuit of my best life. I am never alone when taking brave action. My brave acts are always encouraged and supported by God.

"In whom we have boldness and access with confidence
by the faith of him"
Ephesians 3:12

I am a leader and will use my influence to inspire positivity.

"Let no man despise thy youth; but be thou an
example of the believers, in word, in conversation,
in charity, in spirit, in faith, in purity."
1 Timothy 4:12

_____

_____

_____

_____

_____

_____

_____

_____

_____

_____

_____

_____

I am anointed. I am not a slave to sin. I have been set free. I have God's anointing, and that's what matters. I am a child of the most high God.

_____

_____

_____

_____

_____

_____

_____

_____

_____

_____

_____

_____

_____

"Now he which stablisheth us with you in Christ, and hath anointed us, is God; Who hath also sealed us, and given the earnest of the Spirit in our hearts."
2 Corinthians 1:21-22

_____

_____

_____

_____

_____

_____

_____

_____

_____

_____

_____

_____

I am Strong and powerful. Great strength lies within me at all times.

*"Finally, my brethren, be strong in the Lord, and
in the power of his might."*
Ephesians 6:10

---

*I am Worthy of love and respect. I release the
need for validation from others.*

"Being confident of this very thing, that he which hath begun a good work in you will perform it until the day of Jesus Christ:"
Philippians 1:6

_____

_____

_____

_____

_____

_____

_____

_____

_____

_____

_____

_____

*I am comfortable being myself around others. I am a
unique individual with valuable perspectives*

_____

_____

_____

_____

_____

_____

_____

_____

_____

_____

_____

_____

_____

"For you created my inmost being; you knit me together in my mother's womb. I praise you because I am fearfully and wonderfully made; your works are wonderful, I know that full well."
Psalm 139:13-14

I am Intelligent, setting and achieving ambitious goals.

"I can do all things through Christ who strengthens me."
(Philippians 4:13)

_____

_____

_____

_____

_____

_____

_____

_____

_____

_____

_____

_____

_____

_____

I am Blessed and highly favored. The blessings of the Lord are mine. His favor serves as a covering and a source of divine assistance in my life.

_____

_____

_____

_____

_____

_____

_____

_____

_____

_____

_____

_____

_____

_____

"For You, O Lord, will bless the righteous; with favor
You will surround him as with a shield."
Psalm 5:12

I am God-fearing. I respect, obey, and submit to
God's discipline, worshiping Him in awe.

"The fear of the LORD is the beginning of wisdom:
And the knowledge of the holy is understanding."
Proverbs 9:10

_____

_____

_____

_____

_____

_____

_____

_____

_____

_____

_____

_____

_____

_____

I am fully responsible for my own happiness.

_____

_____

_____

_____

_____

_____

_____

_____

_____

_____

_____

_____

_____

"Happy are the people whose God is the LORD."
Psalm 144:15

_____

_____

_____

_____

_____

_____

_____

_____

_____

_____

_____

_____

_____

_____

I am attracting money and wealth into my life

"But thou shalt remember the LORD thy God: for it is he that giveth thee power to get wealth, that he may establish his covenant which he sware unto thy fathers, as it is this day."
Deuteronomy 8:18
Amazing

_____

_____

_____

_____

_____

_____

_____

_____

_____

_____

_____

_____

I am Focused on my higher purpose

"Set your affection on things above, not on things on the earth."
Colossians 3:2

_____

_____

_____

_____

_____

_____

_____

_____

_____

_____

_____

_____

_____

_____

I am giving myself the love I deserve to have.

_____

_____

_____

_____

_____

_____

_____

_____

_____

_____

_____

_____

"And thou shalt love the Lord thy God with all thy heart, and
with all thy soul, and with all thy mind, and with all thy strength:
this is the first commandment. And the second is like, namely this,
Thou shalt love thy neighbour as thyself.
There is none other commandment greater than these."
Mark 12:30, 31

_____

_____

_____

_____

_____

_____

_____

_____

_____

_____

I am ever-evolving and constantly learning

*"But whoso looketh into the perfect law of liberty, and
continueth therein, he being not a forgetful hearer, but a doer of the
work, this man shall be blessed in his deed."*
James 1:25

I am accountable for my own actions

"He that covereth his sins shall not prosper: but whoso confesseth and forsaketh them shall have mercy."
Proverbs 28:13

_____

_____

_____

_____

_____

_____

_____

_____

_____

_____

_____

_____

_____

I am comfortable and confident in my own skin.

"The fear of man bringeth a snare: But whoso putteth his trust in the LORD shall be safe."
Proverbs 29:25

_____

_____

_____

_____

_____

_____

_____

_____

_____

_____

_____

_____

_____

I am ready for what is to come

_____

_____

_____

_____

_____

_____

_____

_____

_____

_____

_____

_____

_____

"And if I go and prepare a place for you, I will come again, and receive you unto myself; that where I am, there ye may be also."
John 14:3

_____

_____

_____

_____

_____

_____

_____

_____

_____

_____

_____

_____

_____

MEET THE AUTHOR

**PROLIFIC AUTHOR. DYNAMIC SPEAKER.
HUMBLE SERVANT.**

Naomi Green Ward was born in Norfolk, Virginia, and raised in Hampton, Virginia. In her academic career, she matriculated at the Hampton Public Schools, Piedmont Valley Community College, Thomas Nelson Community College, and Regent University. She is the sixth child of the late Bishop Samuel L. Green, Jr. and the late Madam Vivian F. Green. She is a wife, mother, and grandmother. She is an administrator with a dream of becoming an acclaimed author.

Naomi has been shaping young minds for over three decades as a youth leader in her church and her community. Her enthusiasm for young people is so great, she has dedicated a significant amount of her time creating different activities and programs for the young people.

Naomi believes that life should be lived to its fullest. She is channeling her life experiences into her debut book, In Her Own Words. This book is filled with some of the lessons she has learned and pitfalls to avoid. Currently absorbed in her debut work, she finds that she is yet evolving and her life has a wealth of experiences and scenarios that can be helpful to others. Naomi holds a BS in Business from Regent University where she incorporated creative writing into her studies. She is blending events that occurred and academic knowledge with storytelling in her book, set to release this month.

Naomi is available to speak at your next event as she continues to share her story and inspiration to those that will listen.

She has expanded her reach by creating NEW Life. NEW Life is aired weekly on FB Live where she gives helpful life encouragements. To stay updated, follow her at www.neward. org

Made in the USA
Columbia, SC
11 February 2024

31252400R00070